*The Use and Power
of Thought*

By C. W. Leadbeater

Copyright © 2021 Lamp of Trismegistus. All rights reserved. No part of this publication may be reproduced or transmitted in any form or by any means, electronic or mechanical, including photocopying, recording, or by any information storage and retrieval system, without permission in writing from Lamp of Trismegistus. Reviewers may quote brief passages.

ISBN: 978-1-63118-589-2

Esoteric Classics

Other Books in this Series and Related Titles

The Hymns of Hermes by G R S Mead (978-1-63118-405-5)

Clairvoyance and Psychic Abilities by A Besant &c (978-1-63118-403-1)

Gnosis of the Mind by G R S Mead (978-1-63118-408-6)

Rosicrucian Rules, Secret Signs, Codes and Symbols by various (978-1-63118-488-8)

An Outline of Theosophy by C W Leadbeater (978-1-63118-452-9)

Paracelsus, the Four Elements and Their Spirits by M P Hall (978-1-63118-400-0)

Essays on Ancient Magic by Helena P Blavatsky (978-1-63118-535-9)

Essays on the Esoteric Tradition of Karma by A Besant &c (978-1-63118-426-0)

The Use of Evil by Annie Besant (978-1-63118-532-8)

Occult Arts by William Q. Judge (978-1-63118-559-5)

The Alchemical Catechism of Paracelsus by Paracelsus (978-1-63118-513-7)

Alchemy in the Nineteenth Century by Helena P Blavatsky (978-1-63118-446-8)

Qabbalistic Teachings and the Tree of Life by M P Hall (978-1-63118-482-6)

The Historic, Mythic and Mystic Christ by Annie Besant (978–1–63118–533–5)

The Hidden Mysteries of Christianity by Annie Besant (978–1–63118–534–2)

The Brotherhood of Religions by Annie Besant (978–1–63118–563–2)

The Religion of Theosophy by Bhagwan Das (978–1–63118–565–6)

Arcane Formulas or Mental Alchemy by W W Atkinson (978-1-63118-459-8)

The Machinery of the Mind by Dion Fortune (978-1-63118-451-2)

Vision of the Spirit by C. Jinarajadasa (978-1-63118-560-1)

The Leadbeater Reader: A Selection of Occult Essays (978-1-63118-483-3)

Audio versions are also available on Audible, Amazon and Apple

Other Books in this Series and Related Titles

Commentary on the Pymander by G R S Mead (978–1–63118–588–5)

Hypnotism and Mesmerism by Annie Besant (978–1–63118–587–8)

Spirits of Various Kinds by Helena P Blavatsky (978–1–63118–586–1)

The Hidden Language of Symbolism by Annie Besant (978–1–63118–585–4)

Eastern Magic & Western Spiritualism by Henry S Olcott (978–1–63118–584–7)

Spiritual Progress and Practical Occultism by H P Blavatsky (978–1–63118–583–0)

Memory and Consciousness by Besant & Blavatsky (978–1–63118–582–3)

The Origin of Evil by Helena P Blavatsky (978–1–63118–581–6)

The Camp of Philosophy: Studies in Alchemy by Bloomfield (978–1–63118–580–9)

The Testaments of the Twelve Patriarchs (978–1–63118–579–3)

Occult or Exact Science? by Helena P Blavatsky (978–1–63118–578–6)

Occultism, Semi-Occultism & Pseudo Occultism by A Besant (978–1–63118–577–9)

The Fourth-Gospel and Synoptical Problem by G R S Mead (978–1–63118–576–2)

On the Bhagavad-Gita by T Subba Row &c (978–1–63118–575–5)

What Theosophy Does for Us by C W Leadbeater (978–1–63118–574–8)

Spiritual Life for Man by Annie Besant (978–1–63118–573–1)

The Mysteries by Annie Besant (978–1–63118–572–4)

Fundamental Ideas of Theosophy by Bhagwan Das (978–1–63118–571–7)

Dreams: What They Are and Caused by C W Leadbeater (978–1–63118–570–0)

Communication Between Different Worlds by Annie Besant (978–1–63118–569–4)

Animism, Magic and the Omnipotence of Thought by S Freud (978–1–63118–568–7)

Audio versions are also available on Audible, Amazon and Apple

Table of Contents

Introduction...7

The Use and Power of Thought...9

Difficulties in Clairvoyance...33

INTRODUCTION

The word "esoteric" can be difficult to define. Esotericism in general can be seen less as a system of beliefs and more as a category, which encompasses numerous, different systems of beliefs. It's a bit of juxtaposition, since the word "esoteric" indicates something that few people know about, while the term itself broadly covers numerous philosophies, practices, areas of study and belief systems.

In a greater sense, Esotericism acts as a storehouse for secret knowledge, which is often considered ancient (by *tradition, if not by fact),* passed down from generation to generation, in private. At various times in history, simply possessing the knowledge of some of these subjects, was considered illegal and a jailable offence, if discovered. This usually included such general topics as Alchemy, Pharmacology, Qabalah, Hermeticism, Occultism, Ceremonial Magic, Astrology, Divination, Rosicrucianism and so on. Collectively, these areas of study were often referred to as the esoteric sciences.

Sometimes, the outer garment of a subject isn't esoteric, while what is hidden beneath it, is. As an example, Freemasonry isn't necessarily esoteric by nature (at *least not anymore),* but certain signs, passwords and handshakes given to the candidate during their initiation, are in fact, esoteric, in the sense that they are hidden from the general public.

Today, in the twenty-first century, such topics are readily available at bookstores across the country, and numerous mainsteam publishers offer beginners guides and coffee-table volumes on many of these subjects, intended for mass appeal. Books like *"The Secret"* have turned previously arcane topics into household knowledge. All that being the case, however, it isn't to say that there still aren't buried secrets to uncover, ancient wisdom being ignored and forgotten mysteries to be explored. In fact, it is often that we are only able to further our own studies by standing on the shoulders of these disappearing giants.

Lamp of Trismegistus is doing its part to help preserve humanity's esoteric history by making some of these classics available to those students who are seeking to unearth the knowledge of these ancient colossi.

So, be sure to check other titles from our *Esoteric Classics* series, as well as our *Occult Fiction, Theosophical Classics, Foundations of Freemasonry Series, Supernatural Fiction, Paranormal Research Series, Studies in Buddhism* and our *Christian Apocrypha Series.* You can also download the audio versions of most of these titles from Amazon, Apple or Audible, for learning on the go.

THE USE AND POWER OF THOUGHT

Those who are ignorant of Theosophy sometimes suppose it to be merely a system of speculative philosophy. Nothing could be farther from the truth than this; there is nothing in any way speculative about it, for it is founded entirely upon observation of facts, and upon experiments made in connection with the phenomena and the forces of Nature. From its study emerges a practical rule of life — a rule which cannot but affect the thought and action of its students at every moment of their existence. This is chiefly because it involves a study of life as it really is, so that its students become acquainted with the whole of the world in which they live, instead of knowing only the least important part of it. They are led to understand the laws of evolution; and they naturally learn to live intelligently in accordance with those laws, and to take into account the unseen part of the world as well as the infinitesimal portion which is within reach of the limited physical senses.

Of the general nature of the unseen world I have written elsewhere. For the moment, let us concentrate our attention on one of its most striking characteristics — the ready response of the finer types of matter (of which it is constructed) to the influences of human thought and emotion. It is difficult for those who have not studied the subject to grasp the absolute reality of these forces — to understand that they are in every respect as definite in their action upon the finer type of matter as is the power of steam or electricity over physical matter. Every one knows that a man who has at his disposal a large amount of steam power or electrical power can do useful work and produce definite results; but few people know that every man has at his disposal a certain amount of this other and higher power, and that with that he can produce results just as definite and just as real. As matters stand at present in the physical world, only a few men can have at their disposal any large amount of its forces, and so only a few can become rich by their means; but it is a prominent feature of the vivid interest of the unseen side of life, that every human being, rich or poor, old or young, has already at his disposal no inconsiderable proportion of its forces. And therefore the riches of these higher planes, which are obtained by the right use of these powers, are within the reach of all.

Here, then, is a power possessed by all, but intelligently used as yet by few. It is, surely well worth our while to take up the matter, to enquire into it, and to try to comprehend it. Indeed there is even more reason for so doing than has yet been mentioned; for the truth is that to some extent we are all already unconsciously making use of this power, and because of our ignorance we are employing it wrongly, and doing harm with it instead of good. The possession of power always means responsibility; so in order to avoid doing harm unintentionally, and in order to utilize thoroughly these magnificent possibilities, it will clearly be well for us to learn all that we can on this subject.

What, then, is THOUGHT, and how does it show itself? Those who have even a superficial acquaintance with Theosophical literature are aware that man possesses a vehicle corresponding to each of the interpenetrating worlds of our solar system — that his astral body is the vehicle of his desires, passions, and emotions; and that his thought expresses itself through that higher vehicle of still finer matter which we usually call the mental body. It is in this latter vehicle that thought first shows itself to the sight of the clairvoyant; and it appears as a vibration of its matter — a vibration which is found to produce various effects, all of them quite in line with what scientific experience in the physical world would lead us to expect.

First there is the effect produced upon the mental body itself; and we find that to be of the nature of setting up a habit. There are many different types of matter in the mental body, and each of them appears to have its own special rate of oscillation, to which it seems most accustomed, so that it readily responds to it and tends to return thereto as soon as possible when it has been forced away from it by some strong rush of thought or feeling. A sufficiently strong thought may for the moment set the whole of the matter of the mental body swinging at the same rate; and every time that that happens it is a little easier for it to happen again. A habit of vibrating at that rate is being set up in the mental body, so that the man will readily repeat that particular thought.

Secondly, there is the effect produced upon the other vehicles of the man, which are above and below the mental body in degree of density. We know that in the physical world disturbances in one type of matter are readily communicated to another type — that, for example, an earthquake will produce a mighty wave in the sea and again (from the other side) that the disturbance of the air by a storm will immediately produce ripples, and presently great waves, in the ocean beneath it. In just the same way a disturbance in a man's astral body (that is to say, what we commonly call an emotion) will set up undulations in the mental body, and cause thoughts which correspond to the emotion. Conversely, the movement in the mental body affects the astral body, if it be of a type which can affect it — which means that certain types of thought will readily provoke emotion. Just as the mental vibration acts upon the astral matter, which is denser than it is, so also does it inevitably act upon the matter of the causal body, which is finer than it. Thus the habitual thought of the man builds up qualities in the ego himself.

So far, we have been dealing with the effect of the man's thought upon himself; and we see that in the first place it tends to repeat itself, and that in the second place it acts not only upon his emotions, but also permanently upon the man himself. Now let us turn to the effects which it produces outside of himself — that is, upon the sea of mental matter which surrounds us all, just as does the atmosphere.

Thirdly, then, every thought produces a radiating undulation, which may be either simple or complex according to the nature of the thought that gives it birth. This vibration may under certain conditions be confined to the mental world, but also it may produce an effect in worlds above and below. If the thought be purely intellectual and impersonal — if, for example, the thinker is considering a philosophical system, or attempting to solve a problem in algebra or geometry — the wave sent forth will affect merely the mental matter. If the thought be of a spiritual nature, if it be tinged with love or aspiration, or with deep unselfish feeling, it will rise upwards into the realm of the higher mental, and may even borrow some of the splendour and glory of the intuitional level — a combination which renders it exceedingly powerful. If, on the other hand, the thought is tinged with something of self or of personal desire, its oscillations at once draw downwards and expend most of their force in the astral world.

All these undulations act upon their respective levels just as does a vibration of light or sound here in the physical world. They radiate out in all directions, becoming less powerful in proportion to their distance from their source. But we should remember that the radiations affect not only the sea of mental matter which surrounds us, but also act upon other mental bodies moving within that sea. We are all familiar with the experiment in which a note struck on a piano, or a string sounded on a violin, will set the corresponding note sounding upon another instrument of the same kind, which has been tuned exactly to the same pitch. Just as the vibration set up in one instrument is conveyed through the air and acts upon the other instrument, so is the thought-vibration set up in one mental body conveyed by the surrounding mental matter and reproduced in another mental body — which, stated from another point of view, means that thought is infectious. We will return to this consideration later.

Fourthly, every thought produces not only an undulation but a form — a definite, separate object, which is endowed with force and vitality of a certain kind, and in many cases behaves like a temporary living creature. This form, like the vibration, may be in the mental world only; but much more frequently it descends to the astral level and produces its principal effect in the world of emotions. The study of these thought-forms is of exceeding interest; a detailed account of many of them, with coloured illustrations of their appearance, will be found in a book called *Thought-Forms*, which can be had at *The Theosophist Office*. At the moment, we are concerned less with their appearance than with their effects and with the way in which they can be utilized.

Let us consider separately the action of these two manifestations of thought-power. The vibration may be simple or it may be complex, according to the character of the thought; but its strength is poured out chiefly upon some one of the four levels of mental matter — the four subdivisions which constitute the lower part of the mental world. Most of the thoughts of the ordinary man center round himself, his desires, and his emotions, and they are therefore undulations of the lowest subdivision of mental matter; indeed, the corresponding part of the mental body is the only one which is as yet fully developed and active in the great majority of mankind. It must not be forgotten that in this respect the condition of the mental body is very different from that of the astral vehicle. In the ordinary cultured man of our race the astral body is, as fully developed as the physical, and the man is perfectly capable of using it as a vehicle of consciousness. He is not yet much in the habit of so using it, and is consequently shy about it and distrustful of his powers; but the astral powers are all there, and it is simply a question of becoming accustomed to their use. When he finds himself functioning in the astral world either during sleep or after death, he is fully capable of sight and hearing, and can move about whithersoever he will.

In the heaven-world, however, he finds himself under very different conditions, for the mental body is as yet by no means fully developed, that being the part of its evolution upon which the human race is at the present moment engaged. The mental body can be employed as a vehicle only by those who have been specially trained in its use under Teachers belonging to the Great Brotherhood of Initiates; in the average man it is only partially developed, and cannot in the least be employed as a separate vehicle of consciousness. In the majority of men the higher portions of the mental body are as yet quite dormant, even when, the lower portions are in vigorous activity. This necessarily implies that while the whole mental atmosphere is surging with vibrations belonging to the lowest subdivision, there is as yet comparatively little activity on the higher subdivisions — a fact which we shall need to have clearly in mind when we come to consider presently the practical possibility of the use of thought-power. It has also an important bearing upon the distance to which a thought-wave may penetrate.

The distance covered by such a wave, and the strength and persistence with which it can impinge upon the mental bodies of others, depend upon the strength and clearness of the original thought. In this respect it resembles the voice of a speaker, setting in motion waves of sound in the air, which radiate from him in all directions, and convey his words to all those who are (as we say) within hearing; and the distance to which his voice can penetrate depends upon its strength and the clearness of his enunciation. In exactly the same way a strong thought will carry much farther than one which is weak and undecided; but clearness and distinctness are of even greater importance than strength. Again, just as the speaker's voice may fall upon heedless ears where men are already engaged in business or in pleasure, so may a strong wave of thought sweep past without affecting the mind of a man if he is already wholly engrossed in some other line of thought. Many men, however, do not think definitely or strongly except when in the immediate prosecution of some business that demands their whole attention, so that there are always within reach many minds that are liable to be considerably affected by the thoughts which impinge upon them.

The action of this undulation is eminently adaptable. It may exactly reproduce itself, if it finds a mental body which readily responds to it in every particular; but when this is not the case, it may nevertheless produce a decided effect along lines broadly similar to its own. Suppose for example, that a Catholic kneels in devotion before an image of the Blessed Virgin. He sends rippling out from him in all directions strong devotional vibrations; if they strike upon the mental or astral body of another Catholic, they will arouse in him a thought and feeling identical with the original. But if they should strike upon a Christian of some other sect, to whom the image of the Blessed Virgin is unfamiliar, they will still awaken in him the sentiment of devotion, but that will follow along its accustomed channel, and be directed towards the Christ.

In the same way, if they should touch a Muhammadan they would arouse in him devotion to Allah, while in the case of a Hindû the object might be Krshna, and in the case of a Pãrsî, Ahuramazda. But they would excite devotion of some sort wherever there was a possibility of response to that idea. If, however, they should touch the mental body of a materialist, to whom the very idea of devotion in any form is unknown, they would still produce an elevating effect. They could not at once create a type of vibration to which the man was wholly unaccustomed, but their tendency would be to stir a higher part of his mental body into some sort of activity; and the effect, though less permanent than in the case of the sympathetic recipient, could not fail to be good.

The action of an evil or impure thought is governed by the same laws. A man who is so foolish as to allow himself to think of another with hatred or envy radiates a wave tending to provoke similar passions in others; and though his feeling of hatred be for someone quite unknown to these others, and so it is impossible that they should share it, yet the radiation will stir in them an emotion of the same nature towards a totally different person.

The work of the thought-form is more limited, but much more precise than that of the undulation. It cannot reach so many persons — indeed we may say that it cannot act upon a person at all unless he has in him something which is harmonious with the vibrant energy which ensouls it. The powers and possibilities of these thought-forms will perhaps be clearer to us if we attempt to classify them. Let us consider first the thought which is definitely directed towards another person — as when a man sends forth from himself a thought of affection or of gratitude (or unfortunately it may be sometimes of envy or jealousy) towards someone else. Such a thought will produce radiating waves precisely as would any other, and will therefore tend to reproduce itself in the minds of those within the sphere of its influence. But the thought-form which it creates is imbued with definite intention, as it were; and as soon as it breaks away from the mental and astral bodies of the thinkers it goes straight towards the person to whom it is directed, and fastens itself upon him.

It may be compared not inaptly to a Leyden jar with its charge of electricity — the matter of the mental and astral worlds forming the body, which is symbolized by the jar, and the vibrant energy of the thought which ensouls it corresponding to the charge of electricity. If the man towards whom it is directed is at the moment in a passive condition, or if he has within him active oscillations of a character harmonious with its own, it will at once discharge itself upon him. Its effect will naturally be to provoke an undulation similar to its own if none such previously existed, and to intensify it if it is already to be found there. If the man's mind is for the time so strongly occupied along some other lines that it is impossible for the vibration to find an entrance, the thought-form hovers about him waiting for an opportunity to discharge itself.

In the case of a thought which is not directed to some other person, but is connected chiefly with the thinker himself (as indeed are the majority of man's thoughts), the undulation spreads in all directions as usual, but the thought-form floats in the immediate neighbourhood of its creator, and its tendency is constantly to react upon him. As long as his mind is fully occupied with business, or with a thought of some other type, the floating form simply bides its time; but when his train of thought is exhausted, or his mind for a moment lies fallow, it has an opportunity to react upon him, and immediately it begins to repeat itself — to stir up in his mind a repetition of the thought to which he has previously yielded himself. Many a man may be seen surrounded by a shell of such thought-forms, and he will frequently feel their pressure upon him — a constant suggestion from without of certain thoughts; and if the thought be evil, he very likely believes himself to be tempted by the devil: whereas the truth is that he is his own tempter, and that the evil thoughts are entirely his own creation.

Thirdly, there is the class of thought which is neither centered round the thinker nor aimed specially at any person. The thought-form generated in this case does not hang about the thinker, nor has it any special attraction towards another man, so it simply remains idly floating where it was called into existence. Each man as he moves through life is thus producing three classes of thought-forms — those which shoot straight out away from him, aiming at a definite objective; those which hover round him and follow him wherever he goes; and those which he leaves behind him as a sort of trail which marks his route.

The whole atmosphere is filled with thought of this third type, vague and indeterminate; so that as we walk along we are, as it were, picking our way through vast masses of them; and if our minds are not already definitely occupied, these vague wandering fragments of other people's thought will seriously affect us. They, sweep through the mind which is lying idle, and probably the majority of them do not arouse in it any especial interest; but now and then comes one which attracts attention, and the mind fastens upon it, entertains it for a moment or two, and dismisses it a little stronger than it was on arrival. Naturally this mixture of thought from many sources has no definite coherence — though it must be remembered that any one of these may start a line of associated ideas, and so set the mind thinking on its own account. If a man pulls himself up suddenly as he walks along the street, and asks himself: " What am I thinking about, and why ? How did I reach this particular point in my train of thought ?" and if he tries to follow back the line of his thoughts for the last ten minutes, he will probably be quite surprised to discover how many idle and useless thoughts have passed through his mind in that space of time. They are not one-fourth of them his own thoughts; they are simply those fragments which he has picked up as he passed along. In most cases they are quite valueless, and their general tendency is distinctly more likely to be evil than good.

Now that we understand to some extent the action of thought, let us see what use it is possible to make of this knowledge, and what practical considerations emerge from it. Knowing these things, what can we do to forward our own evolution, and what can we do to help others ? Obviously, a scientific consideration of the way in which thought works exhibits it as a matter of far greater importance for evolution than we ordinarily suppose. Since every thought or emotion produces a permanent effect by strengthening or weakening a tendency, and since, furthermore, every thought-vibration and thought- form must inevitably react upon the thinker, the greatest care must be exercised as to the thought or emotion which the man permits within himself. The ordinary man rarely thinks of attempting to check an emotion; when he feels it surging within him he yields himself to it and considers it merely natural. One who studies scientifically the action of these forces realizes that it is his interest as well as his duty to check every such upwelling, and consider before he allows it to sway him whether it is or is not prejudicial to his evolution.

Instead of allowing his emotions to run away with him he must have them absolutely under control; and since the stage of evolution at which we have arrived is the development of the mental body, he must take this matter also seriously in hand and see what can be done to assist that development. Instead of allowing the mind to indulge in its vagaries he should endeavour to assert control over it, recognizing that the mind is not the man, but is an instrument which the man must learn to use. It must not be left to lie fallow; it must not be allowed to remain idle, so that any passing thought-form can drift in upon it and impress it. The worthy Dr. Watts long ago remarked that " Satan finds some mischief still for idle hands to do," and certainly there is truth in the saying when it is applied to these higher levels, for the mind which is left unoccupied is far more likely to take up evil impressions than good ones. The first step towards control of the mind is to learn to keep it usefully occupied — to have some definite good and useful set of thoughts as a background to the mind's operation — something upon which it shall always fall back when there is no immediate need for its activity in connection with duty to be done.

Another most necessary point in its training is that it shall be taught to do thoroughly that which it has to do — in other words, that the power of concentration shall be acquired. This is no light task, as any unpracticed person will find who endeavours to keep his mind absolutely upon one point even for five minutes. He will find that there is an active tendency to wander — that all kinds of other thoughts thrust themselves in; the first effort to fix the mind on one subject, for five minutes is likely to resolve itself into spending five minutes in bringing the mind back again and again from various side-issues which it has followed. Fortunately, though concentration itself is no easy thing, there are plenty of opportunities for attempting it, and the acquisition of it will be of great use in our daily life. We should learn then, whatever we are doing, to focus our attention upon it, and to do it with all our might and as well as it can be done; if we write a letter, let that letter be well and accurately written, and let no carelessness in detail delay it or mar its effect; if we are reading a book, even though it be only a novel, let us read it with attention, trying to grasp the author's meaning, and to gain from it all that there is to be gained. The endeavour to be constantly learning something, to let no day pass without some definite exercise of the mind, is a most salutary one; for it is only by exercise that strength comes, and thus disuse means always weakness and eventual atrophy.

Another point of great importance is that we should learn to husband our energy. Each man possesses only a certain amount of energy, and he is responsible for its utilization to the best advantage. The ordinary man wastes his force in the most foolish manner; but it is especially necessary for the student of occultism to learn to avoid this. The average man is simply a center of agitated vibration; he is constantly in a condition of worry, of trouble about something, or in a condition of deep depression, or else he is unduly excited in the endeavour to grasp something. For one reason or another he is always in a state of unnecessary agitation, usually about the merest trifle. Although he never thinks about it, he is all the while influencing other people around him by this condition of his astral and mental bodies; he is constantly communicating these vibrations and this agitation to those unfortunate people who are near him. It is just because millions of people are thus unnecessarily agitated by all sorts of foolish desires and feelings that it is difficult for a sensitive person to live in a large city, or to go into a great crowd of his fellow-men.

Another way in which the average man wastes a great deal of force is by unnecessary argument. It appears to be impossible for him to hold any opinion, whether it be religious or political, or relating to some matter in ordinary life, without becoming a prey to an overmastering desire to force this opinion upon everyone else. He seems quite incapable of grasping the rudimentary fact that what another man chooses to believe is no business of his, and that he is not commissioned by the authorities in charge of the world to go round and secure uniformity in thought and practice. The wise man realizes that truth is a many-sided thing, not commonly held in its entirety by any one man, or by any one set of men; he knows that there is room for diversity of opinion upon almost any conceivable subject, and that therefore a man whose point of view is opposite to his own may nevertheless have something of reason and truth in his belief, He knows that most of the subjects over which men argue are not in the least worth the trouble of discussion, and that those who speak most loudly and most confidently about them are usually those who know least. The student of occultism will therefore decline to waste his time in argument; if he is asked for information he is quite willing to give it, but not to waste his time and strength in unprofitable wrangling.

Another painfully common method of wasting strength is in worry. Many men are constantly forecasting evil for themselves and for those whom they love — troubling themselves with the fear of death and of what comes after it, with the fear of financial ruin or loss of social position. A vast amount of strength is frittered away along these unprofitable and unpleasant lines; but all such foolishness is swept aside for the man who realizes that the world is governed by a law of absolute justice, that progress towards the highest is the Divine Will for him, that he cannot escape from that progress, that whatever comes in his way and whatever happens to him is meant to help him along that line, and that he himself is the only person who can delay that advance. He no longer troubles and fears about himself and about others; he simply goes on and does the duty that comes nearest in the best way that, he can, confident that if he does that, all will be well for him. He knows that worry never yet helped anyone, nor has it ever been of the slightest use, but that it has been responsible for an immense amount of evil and waste of force.

The wise man declines to spend his strength in ill-directed emotion. For example, he will utterly decline to take offence at what is said or done by someone else. If another man says something which is untrue or offensive, it is certain that in nine cases out of ten there was no evil intention behind the remark, so that it is not only foolish but unjust to be disturbed about it. Even in the rare case where the remark is intentionally wicked and spiteful — where the man said something purposely to wound another — it is still utterly foolish for that other to allow himself to feel hurt. The irritating word does not in any way injure him, except in so far as he may choose to take it up and injure himself by brooding over it or allowing himself to be wounded in his feelings. What are the words of another, that he should let his serenity be disturbed by them ? If he permits himself to care about what another, has said, then it is he himself who is responsible for the disturbance created in his mental body, and not the other man. The other has done and can do nothing that can harm him, and if the student feels hurt and injured, and thereby makes a great deal of trouble for himself, he has only himself to thank for it. If he suffers a disturbance to arise within his mental body or his astral body in reference to something that another has said, that is merely because he has not yet perfect control over his vehicles; he has not yet developed the common-sense which enables him to look down as a soul upon all this, and to go on his way and attend to his own work without taking the slightest notice of foolish or spiteful remarks made by others.

But this is after all only one side of the matter, and that the least important. It is certainly necessary for his own evolution that man should keep mind and emotion under control, and not foolishly waste his force; but it is assuredly still more necessary from another point of view, because it is only by such care that he can enable himself to be of use to his fellow-men, that he can avoid doing harm to them and can learn how to do good. If, for example, he lets himself feel angry, he naturally produces a serious effect upon himself, because he sets up an evil habit and makes it more difficult to resist the evil impulse next time it assails him. But he also acts seriously upon others around him, for inevitably the vibration which radiates from him must affect them also. If he is making an effort to control his irritability, so perhaps are they, and his action will help or hinder them, even though he is not in the least thinking of them. Every time that he allows himself to send out a wave of anger, that tends to arouse a similar vibration in the mind or astral body of another — to arouse it if it has not previously existed, and to intensify it if it is already present; and thus he makes his brother's work of self-development harder for him, and places a heavier burden upon his shoulders. On the other hand, if he controls and represses that wave of anger, lie radiates instead calming and soothing influences which are distinctly helpful to all those near him who are engaged in the same struggle.

Inevitably and without any effort of ours any thought which arises within our minds must be influencing the minds of others about us. Consider then the responsibility if a thought be impure or evil, for we are then spreading moral contagion among our fellow-men. Hundreds and thousands of people possess within them latent germs of evil — germs which may never blossom and bear fruit unless some force from without plays upon them and stirs them into activity. If we yield ourselves to an impure or unholy thought, the wave of force which we thus produce may be the very factor which awakens the germ and causes it to begin to grow, and so we may start some soul upon a downward career. The impulse so given may blossom out later into thoughts and words and deeds of evil, and these in their turn may injuriously affect thousands of other men even in the far distant future. We see then how terrible is the responsibility of a single impure or evil thought. Happily all this is true of good thought as well as of evil, and the man who realizes this may set himself to work to be a veritable sun, constantly radiating upon all his neighbours thoughts of love and calm and peace. This is a truly magnificent power, yet it is within the reach of every human being, of the poorest as well as the wealthiest, of the little child as well as the great sage.

Possessing this tremendous power, we must be careful how we exercise it. We must remember to think of a person as we wish him to be, for the image that we thus make of him will naturally act powerfully upon him and tend to draw him gradually into harmony with itself. Let us fix our thoughts upon the good qualities of our friends, because in thinking of any quality we tend to strengthen its undulations, and therefore to intensify it.

From this consideration it follows that the habit of gossip and scandal, in which many people thoughtlessly indulge themselves, is in reality a horrible wickedness, in condemning which no expression can be too strong. When people are guilty of the impertinence of discussing others, it is not usually upon the good qualities that they most insist. We have therefore a number of people fixing their thought upon some alleged evil in another, calling to that evil the attention of others who might perhaps not have observed it; and in this way, if that bad quality really exists in the person whom they are so improperly criticizing, they distinctly increase it by strengthening the vibration which is its expression. If, as is usually the case, the depravity exists only in their own prurient imagination, and is not present in the person about whom they are gossiping, then they are doing the utmost in their power to create that evil quality in that person, and if there be any latent germ of it existing in their victim, their nefarious effort is only too likely to be successful.

Assuredly we may think helpfully of those whom we love; we may hold before them in thought a high ideal of themselves, and wish strongly that they may presently be enabled to attain it. If we know of certain defects or vices in a man's character we should never under any circumstances let our thoughts dwell upon them and intensify them; on the contrary we should formulate a strong thought of the contrary virtues, and then send out waves of that thought to the man who needs our help. The ordinary method is for one to say to another:

"O my dear, what a terrible thing it is that Mrs. So-and-So is so ill-tempered! Why, do you know, only yesterday she did this and that, and I have heard that she constantly, etc., etc.. Isn't it a terrible thing?

And this is repeated by each person to her thirty or forty dearest friends, and in a few hours several hundred people are pouring converging streams of thought, all about anger and irritability, upon the unfortunate victim. Is it any wonder that she presently justifies their expectations, and gives them yet another example of ill-temper over which they can gloat?

A man wishing to help in such a case will be especially careful to avoid the idea of anger, but will think with all his force: " I wish Mrs. So-and-So were calm and serene; she has the possibility of such self- control within her; let me try frequently to send her a strong calm soothing influence, such as will help her to realize the Divine possibility within her". In the one case the thought is of anger, and in the other case it is of serenity; in both alike it will inevitably find its goal, and tend to reproduce itself in the mental and astral bodies of the person of whom the thought is made. By all means let us think frequently and lovingly of our friends, but let us think of their good points, and try by concentrating our attention upon those to strengthen them and to help our, friends by their means; let our criticism be of that happy kind which grasps at a pearl as eagerly as the criticism of the average man pounces upon an imaginary flaw.

A man will often say that he cannot control his thought or his passion, that he has often tried to do so, but has constantly failed, and has therefore come to the conclusion that such effort is useless. This idea is wholly unscientific. If an evil quality or habit possesses a certain amount of strength within us, it is because in previous lives we have allowed that strength to accumulate — because we have not resisted it in the beginning, when it could easily have been repressed, but have permitted it to gather the momentum which makes it difficult now to deal with it.

We have in fact, made it very easy for ourselves to move along a certain line, and correspondingly difficult to move along another line — difficult, but not impossible. The amount of momentum or energy accumulated is necessarily a finite amount; even if we have devoted several lives entirely to storing up such energy (an unlikely supposition), still the time so occupied has been a limited time, and the results are necessarily finite. If we have now realized the mistake we made, and are setting ourselves to control that habit and to counteract that impetus, we shall find it necessary to put forth exactly as much strength in the opposite direction as we originally spent in setting up that momentum. Naturally we cannot instantly produce sufficient force entirely to counteract the work of many years, but every effort which we make will reduce the amount of force stored up. We ourselves as living souls can go on generating force indefinitely; we have an infinite store of strength on which to draw, and therefore it is absolutely certain that if we persevere we must eventually succeed. However often we may fail, each time something is withdrawn from that finite store of force, and it will be exhausted before we shall, so that our eventual success is simply a matter of mechanics.

You may have seen a railway porter, by steady and continuous pushing, set a big wagon or carriage in motion. Having brought it where he wishes, how does he stop it? It is quite impossible for him, even by the exertion of his utmost strength, to check it instantaneously; so he puts himself in front of it and pushes vigorously against it, walking backwards as its advance forces him along, but never ceasing to exert his force against that advance. Thus by degrees he counterbalances the momentum which he has himself produced in it, and so at last wins his victory and brings it to rest. A good object-lesson in the neutralization of previous karma!

The knowledge of the use of these thought-currents makes it possible for us always to give assistance when we know of some case of sorrow or suffering. It very often happens that we are unable to do anything for the sufferer in the physical world; our physical presence may not be helpful to him; his physical brain may be closed to our suggestions by prejudice or by religious bigotry. But his astral and mental bodies are far more easily impressible than the physical, and it is always open to us to approach these by a wave of helpful thought or of affection and soothing feeling.

We must not forget that the law of cause and effect holds good just as certainly in finer matter as in denser, and that consequently the energy which we pour forth must reach its goal and must produce its effect. There can be no question that the image or the idea which we wish to put before a man for his comfort or his help will reach him; whether it will present itself clearly to his mind when it arrives, depends first upon the definiteness of outline which we have been able to give to it, and secondly upon his mental condition at the time. He may be so fully occupied with thoughts of his own trials and sufferings that there is little room for our idea to insert itself; but in that case our thought-form simply bides its time, and when at last his attention is diverted, or exhaustion forces him to suspend the activity of his own train of thought, assuredly ours will slip in and will do its errand of mercy. There are so many cases where the best will in the world can do nothing physically for a sufferer; but there is no conceivable case in which in either the mental or the astral world some relief cannot be given by steady concentrated loving thought.

The phenomena of mind-cure show how powerful thought may be even in the physical world, and since it acts so much more easily in astral and mental matter we may realize vividly how tremendous the power really is, if we will but exercise it. We should watch for an opportunity of being thus helpful; there is little doubt that plenty of cases will offer themselves. As we walk along the street, as we ride in a tram-car or a railway train, we may often see someone who is obviously suffering from depression or sadness; there is our opportunity, and we may immediately take advantage of it by trying to arouse and to help him. Let us try to send him strongly the feeling that in spite of his personal sorrows and troubles the sun still shines above all, and there is still much for which to be thankful, much that is good and beautiful in the world.

Sometimes we may see the instant effect of our effort — we may actually watch the man brighten up under the influence of the thought which we have sent to him. We cannot always expect such immediate physical result; but if we understand the laws of nature we shall in every case be equally sure that some result is being produced.

It is often difficult for the man who is unaccustomed to these studies to believe that he is really affecting those at whom his thought is aimed; but experience in a great number of cases has shown us that anyone who makes a practice of such efforts will in time find evidence of his success accumulating until it is no longer possible for him to doubt. Each man should make it part of his life thus to try to help all whom he knows and loves, whether they be what is commonly called living or what is commonly called dead; for naturally the possession or the absence of the physical body makes no difference whatever to the action of forces which are leveled at the mental and astral bodies. By steady regular practice great good will be done, for we again strength by using it, and so while we are developing our own powers and ensuring our progress the world will be helped by our kindly efforts.

I remember seeing in an American book on mind-cure a passage which illustrates exceedingly well what should be the Theosophical attitude with regard to the duties and associations of daily life:

"Knead love into the bread you bake", it ran; "wrap strength and courage in the parcel which you tie for the woman with the weary face; hand trust and candour with the coin that you pay to the man with the suspicious eyes".

Quaint in expression, but lovely in its thought; truly the Theosophical concept that every connection is an opportunity, and that everyone whom we meet even casually is a person to be helped. Thus the student of the Good Law goes through life distributing blessings on all about him, doing good unobtrusively everywhere, though often the recipients of the blessing and the help may have no idea whence it comes. Never forget that in such benefactions every man can take his share, and every man ought to take his share; all who can think can send out kindly helpful thoughts, and no such thought has ever failed, or can ever fail while the laws of the universe hold. We may not always see the result, but the result is there, and we know not what fruit may spring from the tiny seed which we sow in passing along our path of Peace and Love.

DIFFICULTIES IN CLAIRVOYANCE

In the early days of the Theosophical Society there was an impression current among us that psychic powers could not be developed except by one who from birth had possessed a physical vehicle of suitable type - that some people were psychic by nature, in consequence of efforts made in previous lives, and that others, who were not so favoured, had no resource but to devote themselves earnestly to what-ever, physical-plane work they could do, in the hope that they might thereby earn the privilege of being born with a psychic vehicle next time. The fuller knowledge of later years has to some extent modified this idea; we see now that under certain stimuli any ordinarily refined vehicle will unfold some portion of psychic capacity, and we have come to be by no means so sure as we used to be, that the possession of psychic faculties from birth is really an advantage. It is quite clear that it is an advantage in some ways, and that it ought to be an advantage in all; but as a matter of experience it often brings with it serious practical difficulties.

The boy who has it, knows a world from which his less fortunate fellows are excluded - a world of gnomes and fairies, of actual comradeship with animals and birds, with trees and flowers, of living sympathy with all the moods of nature - a world freer, less sordid and far more real than the dull round of everyday life. If he has the good fortune - the very rare good fortune - to have sensible parents, they sympathise with him in all this, and explain to him that this fairy world of his is not a separate one, but only the higher and more romantic part of the life of the gracious and marvellous old earth to which we belong, and that therefore everyday life, when properly understood, is not dull and grey, but instinct with vivid wonder and joy and beauty.

There can be no question of the advantage here; but, unfortunately, as I have just said, the sensible parent is rare, and the budding poet, artist or mystic is quite likely to find himself in the hands of an unsympathetic bourgeoisie, wholly incapable of comprehending him, and thoroughly permeated with fear and hatred of anything which is sufficiently unusual to rise a little above the level of the deadly dullness of their smug respectability. Then is his lot indeed unhappy; he soon learns that he must live a double life, carefully hiding the romantic realities from the rude jeers of the ignorant Philistine, and but too often the crass brutality of this most reprehensible repression stifles altogether the dawning perception of the spirit and drives him back into his shell for this incarnation. Hundreds of valuable clairvoyants are thus lost to the world, merely through the unconscious cruelty of well-meaning stupidity.

Some boys, however, and perhaps still more often some girls, do not entirely lose their powers, but bring through some fragments of them into adult life; and not improbably the very fact that they have thus direct knowledge of the existence of the unseen world, draws them to the study of Theosophy. When that happens, is their psychism an advantage to them?

There is no doubt that it ought to be. Not only do they know as a fact of experience many things which other students accept merely as a necessary hypothesis, but they can also understand far better than others all descriptions of higher conditions of consciousness - descriptions which, because they are couched in physical language, must necessarily be woefully imperfect. The clairvoyant cannot doubt the life after death, because the dead are often present to him; he cannot question the existence of good and evil influences, for he daily sees and feels them.

Thus there are many ways in which clairvoyance is an incalculable benefit. On the whole, I think that it makes happier the life of its possessor; it enables him to be more useful to his fellows than he could otherwise be. If balanced always by common sense and humility, it is indeed a most excellent gift; if not so balanced, it may lead to a good deal of harm, for it may deceive both the clairvoyant himself and those who trust in him. Not if proper care is exercised; but many people do not exercise proper care, and so inaccuracy arises.

Especially is this the case when the operator endeavours to use the powers of the higher vehicles, because in the first place, long and careful training is needed before these can be rightly used, and secondly the results must be brought down through several intermediate vehicles, which offer many opportunities for distortion. A good example of the kind of work in question is the investigation of past history or of the previous lives of an individual - what is commonly called examining the records. In order to obtain reliable results, this must be done through the causal body; and to chronicle the observations correctly on this lower plane we must have four vehicles thoroughly under control - which is a good deal to expect.

The physical body must be in perfect health, for if it is not, it may produce the most extraordinary illusion and distortions. A trifling indigestion, the slightest alteration in the normal circulation of the blood through the brain, either as to quantity, quality or speed, may so alter the functioning of that brain as to make it an entirely unreliable transmitter of the impressions conveyed to it. A similar effect may be produced by any change in the normal volume or velocity of the currents of vitality which are set flowing through the human body by the spleen. The brain mechanism is a complicated one, and unless both the etheric part of it through which the vitality flows and the denser matter which receives the circulation of the blood, are working quite normally, there can be no certainty of a correct report; any irregularity in either part may readily so dull or disturb its receptivity as to produce blurred or distorted images of whatever is presented to it.

The astral body, too, must be perfectly under control, and that means much more than one would at first suppose, for that vehicle is the natural home of desires and emotions, and in most people it is habitually in a condition of wild excitement. What is wanted is not at all what we ordinarily call calmness; it is a far higher degree of tranquillity which is only to be obtained by long training. When a man describes himself as calm, he means only that he has not at the moment any strong feeling in his astral body; but he has always a quantity of smaller feelings which are still keeping up a motion in the vehicle - the swell which still remains, perhaps, after some gale of emotion which swept over him yesterday. But if he wishes to read records or to perform magical ceremonies, be must learn to still even that.

The old simile of the reflection of a tree in a lake can hardly be bettered. When the surface of the water is really still, we have a perfect image of the tree; we can see every leaf of it; we can observe correctly its species and its condition; but the slightest puff of wind shatters that image at once, and creates ripples which so seriously interfere with the image that not only can we no longer count the visible leaves but we can hardly tell even what kind of tree it is, an oak or an elm, an ash or a hornbeam, whether its foliage is thick or thin, whether it is or is not in flower. In fact, our interpretation of the image would, under such conditions, be largely guesswork. And that, be it remembered, is the effect of a mere zephyr; a stronger wind would make everything utterly unintelligible.

The normal condition of our astral bodies might be represented by the effects of a brisk breeze, and our ordinary calmness by the ripplings of a light but persistent air; the mirror-like surface can be attained only after long practice and much strenuous effort. When we realise that for a reliable reading of the records we must reach that condition of perfect placidity not in one vehicle only, but in four, no one of which is ever normally quiet even for a moment, we begin to see that we have a difficult task before us, even if this were all.

Not only must the astral body be tranquil before the investigation is begun, but it must remain unruffled all through the work - which means that, if he wants to get more than a general impression, the seer must not allow himself to be excited by anything which may appear in the picture. Be it observed that the nature of the excitement makes no difference; if a spasm of anger, of fear, is fatal to accuracy, so also is a rush of affection or devotion. If he is to be rigorously truthful, the watcher must record what he sees and hears as impartially as does a camera or a phonograph; he may allow himself the luxury of emotions afterwards when recalling what he has seen, but at the time he must be absolutely impassive, if he is to be reliable. This makes it practically impossible for the emotional or hysterical person to be a trustworthy observer on these higher planes; he surrounds himself with a world of forms built by his own thoughts and feelings, and then proceeds to see and to describe those as though they were external realities.

Often such forms are beautiful, and their contemplation is uplifting, so that, even though they are in-accurate they may be of great help to the seer. Indeed, his experiences may be useful to others also, if he has the discrimination to relate them without labelling his actors as deities, archangels or adepts. But it is usually precisely such figures as those that his imagination evokes, and it is merely human nature to feel that the person who comes to him must surely be some Great One. The only way to secure oneself against self-deception is the old and irksome way of a long, hard course of careful training; except by some vague intuition a man cannot know a thought-form from a reality until he has been taught their respective characteristics, and can rise sufficiently above them to be able to apply his tests.

Calmness is necessary in the mental body as well as the astral. A man who worries can never see accurately, because his mental body is in a condition of chronic disease, a perpetual inflammation of agitated fluttering. One who suffers from pride or ambition has a similar difficulty. Some have supposed that it matters little what they think habitually, so long as during the actual investigation they try to hold their minds still; but that idea is fallacious. In this vehicle, also, the storm of yesterday leaves a swell behind it; an attitude of mind which is constantly or frequently held, makes an indelible mark upon the body, and keeps up a steady pulsation of which the owner is as unconscious as he is of the beating of his heart. But its presence becomes obvious when clairvoyance is attempted, and makes anything like clear vision impossible - all the more since the man, being ignorant of its existence, makes no effort to counteract its effects.

Prejudice, again, is an absolute bar to accuracy; and we know how few people are entirely without prejudices. In many cases these mental attitudes are matters of birth and long custom - the attitude, for example, of the average Brahmana to a pariah, or the average American to a negro. Neither of those could report accurately a scene in which appeared any members of the classes they instinctively despise. I may give an example which came under my notice some time ago. I knew a good clairvoyant with strong Christian proclivities. So long as we were dealing with indifferent subjects, her vision was clear; but the moment that anything arose which touched, however remotely, upon her religious beliefs she was instantly up in arms, and became absolutely unreliable. Being a highly intelligent person in many directions, she would have checked this prejudice if she had been conscious of it; but she was not, and so its evil influence was unrestrained. If, for example, a scene rose before us in which a Christian and a man of some other religion came in any way into conflict or even appeared side by side, her description of it was a mere travesty of the reality, for she could see only the good points in the Christian and only the evil in the other man. If any fact appeared which did not fit in with the alleged history contained in the Christian Scriptures, that fact was ignored or distorted to suit her preconceptions; and all this with entire unconsciousness, and with the best possible intentions. That is only one small sample of the unreliability of spontaneous, untrained clairvoyance.

No wonder that it takes many years of patient and careful training before the pupil of the Master can be accepted as really reliable. He must discover all these unrecognised prejudices, and must eliminate them; he must evict from the recesses of his own consciousness other tenants even more firmly attached to the soil - pride, self-consciousness, self-centredness.

This last is a condition from which many people suffer. I do not mean that they are selfish in the ordinary gross meaning of the word; they are often far from that, and they may be kind-hearted, self-sacrificing, anxious to help. Nor do I mean that they are offensively proud or conceited; but just that they like to be under the limelight, to be always well on view in the centre of the stage. Suppose such a person to be psychic from birth; in every case where there is a personal experience to be related, that psychic will necessarily and inevitably magnify his or her personal part in the affair, and that without the slightest intention of doing so.

We know that it sometimes happens that a beginner in astral work identifies himself, in his recollection of some event, with the person whom he has helped. If he had during the night been assisting a man who was killed in a railway accident, he might wake in the morning remembering a dream in which he had been killed in a railway accident, and so on. In something the same way, when the self-centred psychic comes across in his investigations some one with a fine aura, he immediately remembers himself with such an aura; if he sees some one conversing with a Great One, he promptly imagines himself to have had such a conversation, and (without the slightest intention of deceit) invents all sorts of flattering remarks as having been addressed to him by that august Being. All this makes him distinctly dangerous, unless he has quite a phenomenal power of self-effacement and self-control.

Members of the Society who have flattering experiences of this sort have been encouraged to send an account of them to the President or to some other trained seer, in order that the facts (if any) may be disentangled from the embroidery, in the hope that such correction may enable them by slow degrees to learn how to winnow the chaff from the wheat. They come with stories of the marvellous initiations through which they have passed, of the great angels and archangels with whom they have familiarly conversed, and the tales are often so wild and so presumptuous that it requires a great fund of patience to deal adequately with them. No doubt it requires a good deal of patience on their part also, for again and again we have to tell them that they have been watching some one else, and have appropriated his deeds to themselves, or that they have magnified a friendly word into an extravagant laudation.

We may easily see that if the self were just a little more prominent, they would not come and ask for explanations, but would hug to their bosoms the certainty that they really had become high Adepts, or had been affably received by the Chieftain of some distant solar system. So we come by easy gradations to those who have angel-guides, who hear divine voices directing them, and are the constant recipients of the most astounding communications. It is no doubt true that in some cases such people have been charlatans, and that in others they have been insane; but I think it should be understood that the majority of them are neither mendacious nor megalomaniac, but that they do really receive these bombastic proclamations from entities of the astral world - usually from quite undistinguished members of the countless hosts of the dead.

It sometimes happens that a preacher, especially if of some obscure sect, becomes a spirit-guide. In the astral world after death, he discovers some of the inner meanings of his religion which he had never seen before, and he feels that if others could see these matters as he now sees them their whole lives would be changed - as indeed they quite probably would. So if he can manage to influence some psychic lady in his flock, he tells her that he has chosen her to be the instrument for the regeneration of the world, and in order to impress her more profoundly, he often thinks it well to represent his revelation as coming from some high source - indeed he usually supposes that it does so come. Generally the teaching and advice which he gives is good as far as it goes, though rather of the copybook heading style of morality.

But to that dead preacher come presently people who will have none of his sage, moral maxims, but want to know how their love affairs will progress, what horse will win a certain race, and whether certain stocks will go up or down. About all such matters our preacher is sublimely ignorant, but he does not like to confess it, reasoning that as these men believe him to be omniscient because he happens to be dead, they will lose faith in his religious teaching if he declines to answer even the most unsuitable questions. So he gravely advises them on these incongruous subjects, and thereby brings much discredit upon communications from the other world in general, and upon his own reputation in particular.

The untrained psychic among ourselves is often put in precisely the same position, and he or she rarely has the courage to say plainly: "I do not know." One of the very first lessons given to us by the Great Teachers is to distinguish clearly between the few facts that we really know and the vast mass of information which we accept on faith or inference. We are taught that to say "I know " is to make a high claim - a claim which none should ever make without personal certainty; men are wiser to adopt the humbler formula with which begin all the Buddhist Scriptures: "Thus have I heard."

The advantage of the pupil who, not having been psychic in the beginning, is afterwards instructed in these matters, lies, I think, in this: that before the attempt is made to develop any such powers, he is trained in selflessness, his prejudices are eradicated, and his astral and mental bodies are brought under control; and so, when the powers come, he has to deal only with the difficulties inherent in their unfolding and their use, and not with a host of others imposed by his own weaknesses. He has learnt to bring his vehicles into order, to know exactly what he can do with them, and to make allowance for any defects which still exist in them; he understands and allows for the action of that part of the personality which is not normally in manifestation - that which has been called by the Psychical Research Society the subliminal self.

When the powers are opened he does not proceed immediately to riot in their unrestrained use; laboriously and patiently he goes through a series of lessons in the method of their employ - a series which may last for years before he is pronounced entirely reliable. An older pupil takes him in hand, shows him various astral objects, and asks him: "What do you see?" He corrects him when in error, and teaches him how to distinguish those things which all beginners confuse; he explains to him the difference between the two thousand four hundred varieties of the elemental essence, and what combinations of them can best be used for various sorts of work; he shows him how to deal with all sorts of emergencies, how to project thought-currents, how to make artificial elementals - all the manifold minutiae of astral work. At the end of all this preparation the aspirant comes out a really capable workman - an apprentice who can understand the Master's instructions, and has some idea of how to set to work to execute the task confided to him.

The person who is born psychic escapes the trouble of developing the powers; but this great gain brings with it its own peculiar temptations. The man knows and sees, from the first, things which others about him do not know and see; and so he often begins to feel himself superior to others, and he has a confidence in the accuracy of his power of sight which may or may not be justified. Naturally he has feelings and emotions which are brought over from past lives, and these grow along with his psychic faculties; so that he has certain preconceptions and prejudices which are to him like coloured glasses through which he has always looked, so that he has never known any other aspect of nature than that which they show him. The bias which these give him seems to him absolutely part of himself, and it is exceedingly hard for him to overcome it and see things at another angle. Ordinarily he is quite unaware that he is all askew, and acts on the hypothesis that he is seeing straight, and that those who do not agree with him are hopelessly inaccurate.

From all this it emerges that those who possess the psychic faculties by nature should exercise them with the greatest care and circumspection. If they wish that their gift shall be helpful and not harmful, they must above all things become utterly selfless: must uproot their prejudices and preconceptions, so as to be open to the truth as it really is; they must flood themselves with the peace that passeth understanding, the peace that abideth only in the hearts of those who live in the Eternal. For these be the prerequisites to accuracy of vision; and even when that is acquired, they have still to learn to understand that which they see. No man is compelled to publish abroad what he sees; no man need try to look up people's past lives or to read the history of aeons long gone by; but if he wishes to do so he must take the precautions which the experience of the ages has recommended to us, or run the terrible risk of misleading, instead of feeding, the sheep which follow him. Even the uninstructed clairvoyant may do much good if he is humble and careful. If he takes for a Master some one who is not a Master (a thing which is constantly happening), the love and devotion awakened in him are good for him; and if in his enthusiasm he can awaken the same feelings in others, they are good for those others also. A high and noble emotion is always good for him who feels it, even though the object of it may not be so great as he is supposed to be. But the evil comes when the erring seer begins to deliver messages from his pseudo-Master, commands which may not be wise, yet may be blindly obeyed because of their alleged source.

How then is the non-clairvoyant student, who as yet sees nothing for himself, to distinguish between the true and the false? The safest criterion of truth is the utter absence of self. When the visions of any seer tend always to the subtle glorification of that seer, they lie open to the gravest suspicion. When the messages which come through a person are always such as to magnify the occult position, importance or title of that person, distrust becomes inevitable, for we know that in all true Occultism the pupil lives but to forget himself in remembering the good of others, and the power which he covets is that which shall make him appear as nothing in the eyes of men.

Psychic powers are widely desired, and many men ask how they can unfold them. Yet is their possession no unmitigated blessing, for at the stage which the world has reached to-day there is more of evil than of good to be seen by the man who looks with unclouded vision over the great mass of his fellow-creatures. So much of sordid struggle, so much of callous carelessness, so much of man's inhumanity to man, which indeed makes countless thousands mourn, and might well make angels weep; so much of the wicked calculated cruelty of the brutal schoolmaster to his shrinking pupil, of the ferocious driver to his far less brutish ox; so much senseless stupidity, so much of selfishness and sin. Well might the great poet Schiller cry:

"Why hast Thou cast me thus into the town of the ever-blind, to proclaim Thine Oracle with the opened sense? Take back this sad clear-sightedness; take from mine eyes this cruel light! Give me back my blindness - the happy darkness of my senses; take back Thy dreadful gift!"

Truly there is another side to the shield, for so soon as one looks away from humanity to the graceful gambols of the jocund nature-spirit or the gleaming splendour of the glorious Angels one realises why, in spite of all, God looked upon the world which He had made, and saw that it was good. And even among men we see an ever-rising tide of love and pitifulness, of earnest effort and noble sacrifice, a reaching upward towards the God from whom we came, an endeavour to transcend the ape and the tiger, and to fan into a flame the faint spark of Divinity within us. For the greatest of all the gifts that clairvoyance brings is the direct knowledge of the existence of the great White Brotherhood, the certainty that mankind is not without Guides and Leaders, but that there live and move on earth Those who, while They are men even as we are, have yet become as Gods in knowledge and power and love, and so encourage us by Their example and Their help to tread the Path which They have trodden, with the sure and certain hope that one day even we also shall be as They. Thus we have certainty instead of doubt; thus we have happiness instead of sorrow; because we know that, not for alone but for the whole humanity of which we are a part, there will some day come a time when we shall wake up after Their likeness, and shall be satisfied with it.

www.ingramcontent.com/pod-product-compliance
Lightning Source LLC
LaVergne TN
LVHW041501070426
835507LV00009B/745